GIRL TALK

The
ULTIMATE
BODY BOOK
FOR GIRLS

Illustrations by Chris Vallo

KENNEBUNKPORT, MAINE

Girl Talk

Copyright © 2021 by Appleseed Press Book Publishers LLC.

This is an officially licensed book by Cider Mill Press Book Publishers LLC. All rights reserved under the Pan-American and International Copyright Conventions.

No part of this book may be reproduced in whole or in part, scanned, photocopied, recorded, distributed in any printed or electronic form, or reproduced in any manner whatsoever, or by any information storage and retrieval system now known or hereafter invented, without express written permission of the publisher, except in the case of brief quotations embodied in critical articles and reviews.

The scanning, uploading, and distribution of this book via the internet or via any other means without permission of the publisher is illegal and punishable by law. Please support authors' rights, and do not participate in or encourage piracy of copyrighted materials.

13-Digit ISBN: 978-1-64643-085-7
10-Digit ISBN: 1-64643-085-9

This book may be ordered by mail from the publisher. Please include $5.99 for postage and handling. Please support your local bookseller first!

Books published by Cider Mill Press Book Publishers are available at special discounts for bulk purchases in the United States by corporations, institutions, and other organizations. For more information, please contact the publisher.

Cider Mill Press Book Publishers
"Where good books are ready for press"
12 Spring Street
PO Box 454
Kennebunkport, Maine 04046
Visit us online! cidermillpress.com

Typography: Barbieri, Brandon Grotesque, Cafeteria, Grenadine MVB, Reklame Script

Printed in China
2 3 4 5 6 7 8 9 0

CONTENTS

Big Changes Ahead

What kind of changes? Well, lots of things.

The first thing you'll notice is that your body is changing. There are bumps where things used to be flat, and hair where things used to be smooth.

You might notice that your feelings are changing. Maybe you don't like the same things you used to, or maybe you feel happy, sad, tired, or grumpy at strange times for no reason.

You might start to see your relationships changing. Some boys might start to act funny around you, and your friends all seem to be going through changes of their own.

Why all these changes? Well, you're growing up and entering a new phase of your life. It can feel a bit like you're caught up in a whirlwind sometimes. Just when it seems like you're getting really good at being a kid, you start to notice little changes in your body. You might start to notice changes in the way you feel about yourself, your family, and your friends. Maybe the grown-ups around you start talking about how you're "on your way to becoming a woman," even though no one even asked if you were done being a girl yet!

Congratulations and welcome to the wonderful world of growing from a kid to an adult, usually called "puberty," although you might call it a pain in the neck. It can be a difficult time, but it can also be very exciting—we promise!

We hope that this book helps guide you through some of the more challenging times ahead. Whether it was a gift or something you found at the bookstore yourself, it's yours now (well, unless you checked it out from the library), and that means you get to read it however you want.

For example, you might have questions that this book can answer, especially about what is going on with your body and what is going to happen next. You can read just the parts that answer those questions, you can read the book from cover to cover, or you can check the index for the subjects you want to know about right now. You can even read this book while you stand on your head if you want to—and if you're good enough at standing on your head! Also, this is just one little book, so we can't possibly answer every question you have. That's why you'll find additional resources in the back of the book. While you're reading, if you find anything that doesn't make sense to you, that makes you feel weird or scared, or that you have questions about, ask a trusted adult in your life that you can talk things over with.

There's one tiny thing you should know about adults, though: even though they've been through puberty already, that doesn't mean they are comfortable with the subject. Just like you, adults may be a little scared about talking about all this stuff. You could try using this book as a starting point in your conversation.

Sometimes just having something in your hands makes getting a conversation going much easier.

While this time may pose some challenges for you, you already have many resources for dealing with the changes that are coming your way. You have people who love you and want to help you make sense of things, you have friends who are experiencing the same things you are and can understand what you're going through, you have past experiences that you've learned from, and you have your own ideas and hopes and dreams to look forward to. All these things will help make the next few years easier for you. Best of luck to you as you begin the journey that will take you from a girl to a woman. You can do it!

1

The Beginner's Guide to Puberty

Feeling confused about all the changes going on inside (and outside) your body? You're not alone. Whether you've already experienced some of the changes in your body that are described in this book, or you are at the very beginning of this process, having the right information can make this time easier, and perhaps just a teensy-weensy bit less stressful.

Puberty happens whether you feel ready for it or not, but (as your teachers have probably already told you many, many times) knowledge is power. Knowing in advance what will be happening to your body can help you get ready for what's ahead. Surprises might be good for birthdays, but they're no fun when you're talking about puberty's big changes.

There's that word again: puberty. It's possible you've been wondering what this "puberty" that your parents, teachers, and friends are talking about is, and what on earth it has to do with you.

Here's the scoop: puberty is the name of the process that your body goes through when it makes the transition from kid to adult. There is growth and change—a lot of it—some of which can be seen from the outside, and some that just happens inside. Often when girls think of puberty and growing older (or what adults call "becoming a woman"), they think of getting their menstrual period. But while starting your period is one of the obvious signs of puberty, there's a lot more to it than that.

❋ Body Changes: Just The Facts, Ma'am

Puberty begins with some action from the pituitary gland. The pituitary gland—which is located just under the base of your brain, in case you were wondering—sends a chemical message to two small glands called the ovaries. In response, your ovaries begin to grow and produce a hormone called estrogen. Hormones are chemicals that act like instructions for your body. While there are a lot of hormones involved in puberty, estrogen is the main puberty hormone for girls, while testosterone is the main puberty hormone for boys.

❋ The Puberty Timeline

Usually, the first sign of the newly released estrogen doing its work is a growth spurt. Your hands and feet will usually grow first, then you will grow taller, your hips will get wider, and your waist will get smaller. Your growth spurt will most likely slow down a little about the time you start your first period, but most girls do still grow an inch or two after their first period.

A bit later—probably during the middle of your growth spurt— you will start the very first stages of breast development. At the beginning of this process, you will develop something known as "breast buds." These are small mounds that form under the nipple and area of darker skin around your nipple (known as the areola). It's common for one breast to start growing before the other. It's also common for your breast buds to hurt a tiny bit in the beginning, but as your breasts start becoming rounder and fuller, this tenderness should go away.

About the time breast development starts, most girls begin to grow pubic hair (hair near and around the vagina). There might not be much hair at first, and it might be straight and very fine. You might also start to grow hair under your arms, or that might happen a bit later. Some girls don't grow underarm hair until the very end of puberty.

You might start to notice a light yellow or white stain on your underwear. This is called vaginal discharge. Vaginal discharge is a normal part of the way your body cleans itself. Vaginal discharge is just one more reason why you need to change your underwear every day.

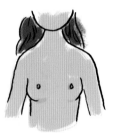

✿ Emotional Changes

Have you ever gotten to the point where you are happy one moment, furious the next, and then sad half an hour later? Welcome to one of the hardest parts of puberty: mood swings.

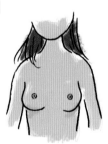

There are at least two reasons for mood swings. The first is the hormonal changes that are going on in your body. Yes, that pesky estrogen strikes again!

The second has to do with your changing place in the world. Puberty is the bridge between being a girl and being a woman, and

sometimes you might feel like you don't belong in either place. You aren't a kid anymore, but sometimes you feel like one inside and still want to do kid things. On the other hand, you aren't ready for the responsibilities that come with being an adult, even though you may feel like you want and need more independence. Some days you might feel out of place and like no one understands what you're going through. No wonder you might be a little (or a lot) cranky!

Talking about your feelings can help keep those emotions in check. Don't worry if it is hard for you to open up—everyone feels this way sometimes. A trusted adult will understand if it is difficult for you to get the words out.

❁ Is That a Breast on My Chest?

Some girls eagerly await breast development and go to sleep with visions of training bras dancing in their heads; other girls might feel like they got busty too early and even feel awkward around other, less developed girls their age. Even though it can be difficult to get breasts before (or after) most people your age, there really is a lot of variation to what is considered normal. Some girls' breasts start developing when they are just nine years old, while other girls might not develop breasts until they are almost 14!

Many girls will start to have breast growth within one year of the time the girl's mother had her first breast development. This is only a rough guess, though, since different factors like nutrition,

health, and exercise can all influence hormone levels, and therefore mean earlier (or later) breast growth.

Having breasts that develop later—or earlier—than the rest of your friends might feel a bit embarrassing. After all, who wants to be different from the rest of the kids in your class? But it will—we promise you—ultimately be OK. Everyone has different bodies, and there is no right or wrong way to grow breasts. You can always talk to a trusted adult or your health care provider if you feel like you've been sitting around forever waiting for your breasts to grow. They can give you a better idea of where you are on the puberty timeline and will probably say you are developing completely normal for you.

Supporting Your Breasts: Bras and Beyond

Once your breasts start developing, the question that girls often wonder about is, "When do I need a bra?" Wearing a bra is mostly a matter of comfort. Some girls like the feeling of support a bra gives them, especially when playing sports or running and jumping. There is no harm in wearing a bra earlier rather than later, but you should talk to the adults in your life about when is the right time for you.

You'll want to take your mom, older sister, or another female adult on your first bra-shopping expedition. Before you go, there are some things that are helpful to know.

First, there are different types of bras. The first bra a girl usually has is a training bra, which doesn't provide a lot of support, but does help you get accustomed to wearing a bra. Some girls find bra-wearing itchy at first, so it's best if a training bra doesn't have much lace or frills to annoy you.

As your breasts get bigger, you might be interested in other types of bras, including some that have wires (covered, of course). These help give some structure to the bra and offer more support. A sports bra is another kind of bra that provides even more support. Sports bras usually fit snugly, so you can run around and play sports without discomfort. You don't have to be into sports to wear a sports bra, though; some girls like how they look and feel and wear them all the time!

Sports bras are sometimes sized as small, medium, and large, but other bras are sized with both a chest size (in the US this is measured in inches) and a cup size. The cup size is usually measured from AA (smallest) to EE (largest).

It is always good to get your bra size measured by an expert. Most bra stores have people called a "lingerie specialist" (which is a fancy way of saying "bra fitter") who are trained to tell you the right bra size for you. They will measure your breasts and around your waist over your T-shirt, and help you pick out a bra that fits best. It's always a good idea to get your bras fitted, so you don't have to fight with a too tight or too loose bra. To test if you have a well-fitting bra, you should be able to comfortably fit two fingers under the bra band (the one that hooks around your back). A bra that is too tight or too loose won't provide any support, and it might even pinch you!

❊ Important Facts About Breasts

- You might have one breast that develops slightly faster than the other breast. This is normal, and you are probably the only one who will notice it.

- Sometimes breasts that develop very quickly will have stretch marks that look like spokes going around the outermost part of the breast. Even if these marks seem easy to see now, they will lighten with time.
- It's normal for your breasts to feel a little achy, sensitive, and heavy in the days right before your period.
- Most experts don't recommend regular breast self-examination for several years because breast problems are very rare in teenage girls, but it's still important to become familiar with the way your breasts look and feel even as they are growing and changing. The best way to do this is by touching your breasts with your fingertips while you are lying down on your back. Push on your breast with the opposite hand using varying levels of pressure (soft and then a little harder) in a circle around your breast. This will help you be aware of any changes later on.
- No one size or shape of breast is healthier than any other size or shape, and having bigger or smaller breasts doesn't increase or decrease your chances of developing breast cancer.
- You should also tell an adult at home or your women's health provider right away if you have any pain in your breasts that

isn't around the time of your period; a red, hot, or swollen area in your breasts; a hard lump that stays the same no matter where you are in your menstrual cycle; or any fluid leaking from your nipple.

❋ Progressing to Your Period

What is commonly called "getting your period" is also known as beginning menstruation. In the simplest terms, menstruation is when a small amount of blood comes out of your vagina over a few days. Although this might sound a little scary, it's a normal process that happens every month to women, starting during puberty and continuing until the age when they can no longer have children.

In order to understand why this happens, we'll need to do a little anatomy review. Girls are born with a place for babies to hang out and grow until they are ready to come into the world. This place is called the uterus. Not too far from the uterus are two glands called the ovaries. The job of the ovaries is to produce estrogen and other hormones, and also to store the eggs that could one day develop into a baby.

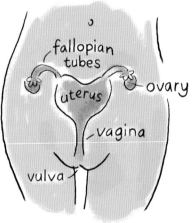

Starting in puberty, about once a month, your ovaries release one of these eggs. The egg travels down a special egg highway (also known as the fallopian tube) that leads from the ovaries to the uterus. This process takes about three days. During the time before the egg reaches the uterus, the lining of the uterus (known as the endometrium) thickens by filling up with blood and fluids. If the egg is fertilized (connects with a sperm to make the very beginning of a baby), the thickened lining is a nice, cozy spot for the fertilized egg to grow into a baby. If the egg arrives in the uterus and is not fertilized, the uterus doesn't need the extra lining it has built up, so it releases the blood and tissue through the vagina over a period of a few days.

❋ Your First Period: How Will You Know?

When you get your period for the first time, you might feel a small amount of liquid coming out of your vagina. Sometimes it's hard to recognize this feeling in the beginning; it's more likely that you will first see something red or rusty-brown on your underwear.

Your first period can be a little surprising even if you know it's coming (one reason for books like this is so girls won't be surprised), but there is no need to panic! Your period won't start flowing heavily all at once, so you have time to get some supplies. If you're away from home and don't have anything with you, you can ask the school nurse (that is, if you're at school) or the mother or grandmother of one of your friends for sanitary products.

Some girls tell all their friends when they get their period, some girls tell just a best friend, and some girls choose to keep it mostly private and maybe only tell their mom and sisters. You should do whatever makes you feel most comfortable. Remember: it's your personal information, and you don't have to share it with anyone, even if they ask. No one can tell by looking at you that you've started your period, even though sometimes it really, really feels like they can! Remember, for most girls and women, having their period is a normal part of their lives, so it's nothing to be ashamed of or grossed out by. Even though some adults don't act like adults about periods, there's nothing gross about having one—it's just a natural part of having a uterus!

Pads vs. Tampons

Here's a comparison between pads and tampons to help you figure out which is right for you.

Where Do They Go?

Tampons: Inserted inside the vagina. Although this may sound gross or difficult to do, most girls get used to it after a few tries. Once a tampon is properly inserted, you can't even tell it is there.

Pads: Attached to your underwear. This is easy to do (and no one will know it is there).

How Often Do You Have to Change Them?

Tampons: It depends on how heavy your flow is, but figure every three to four hours. Be sure to change your tampon at most every six hours, and never sleep in a tampon.

Pads: It depends on how heavy your flow is and how large a pad you use, but figure every three to four hours. There are "overnight" pads that are meant to be worn longer, but you won't want to wear these during the day because they can be somewhat uncomfortable.

What About Sports?

Tampons: Girls who wear tampons often have an easier time participating in sports. You can also go swimming while wearing a tampon.

Pads: Except for swimming, play away! Today's pads are often so thin that you forget that they are there.

Ask your mom or health care provider for more information about pads and tampons. You might also want to try them both to see which is comfortable for you.

During the first few years of having your period, you might feel like it is an exclamation point! Your first periods might be irregular, might start and stop, and might get off track when you're stressed out or  not feeling well. This is common, but by the end of the first year or two of menstruating, most girls will have regular periods. Your menstrual cycle (this is counted as the time from the first day of one period to the first day of the next period) will usually be between 21 and 35 days, though the average is 28 days. A woman's period can typically last from one to seven days. Keeping track of your period on a calendar will help you remember when your period is likely to happen. There are even cool apps to help you keep track of your period once it becomes regular, so you don't have to be caught off guard!

❋ Hey, This Period Is a Pain: PMS and Cramps

Getting your period is a normal, healthy bodily function. You aren't sick when you have your period, and there is no reason to change your daily activities. You can swim, play sports, and do anything else you would normally do, as long as you're comfortable.

Some girls do get cramps that come with their period. These cramps are caused by your uterus contracting as the blood flows out of it. Sometimes girls also get pain in their abdomen or back, nausea, or even a little bit of diarrhea. One of the best treatments for menstrual cramps is heat, either from a warm bath or a heating pad. Exercise helps with cramps during your period too, as does drinking lots of fluids. Over-the-counter pain medications such as ibuprofen can help you continue your daily routine.

Your period shouldn't make it so you feel really sick, or have to take days off from school. If pain relievers don't help, or you get really sick every time your period happens, you should contact a health care provider to see if the cramps are more than just normal period cramps.

During the time of the month right before your period starts, you may have something called premenstrual syndrome (PMS). PMS is caused by changes in your hormones as your body gets ready to start your period. Some girls get moodier during this time. They might feel irritable or might cry more easily, and they might also find they have a craving for certain foods.

Being generally as healthy as possible is the best defense against PMS. Getting some exercise and avoiding caffeine also helps. As for the mood swings, one of the easiest things to do is keep track of your periods on a calendar. That way you'll know when you are due for your period, so if you find yourself crying for absolutely no reason at all, you can at least remember, "Hey, nothing weird is happening here, I've just got PMS."

❊ Your First Visit to Your Gynecologist

Going to the doctor who specializes in the stuff "down there" can be a nerve-wracking experience for a young woman. You most likely won't even need a pelvic exam at your first visit (and you won't need one part of an exam called the pap exam for a few years), but it's important to develop a relationship with a women's health provider. If you need a pelvic exam, here is a brief guide to what you might experience:

- The nurse will show you into an examination room and take your medical history (asking about your periods and stuff like that). The nurse will tell you what items of clothing to remove.

Usually, the nurse gives you a sheet to cover yourself with, so you'll never be totally naked, but if you are feeling anxious about this first exam, ask if you can keep on your T-shirt or wear a robe you've brought from home. If you'd like your mom or another friend to come with you, just ask. Most places don't have a problem with this.

- The table for female examinations often has stirrups at the end of it. These are for you to place your feet in while the doctor examines your vagina and female organs. They may look a bit strange, but the stirrups make it more comfortable for you during the exam.
- The doctor will first examine the outside parts of your vagina and make sure everything has developed normally and is OK. The doctor may then see if it is possible to insert a device (called a speculum) that makes it possible to see inside the vagina. The doctor may also place one or two fingers inside your vagina and one hand on your abdomen. This allows the doctor to feel your ovaries and your uterus. The doctor is looking to make sure they are a normal size and have developed appropriately.

Don't hesitate to ask questions or to hold your mom's hand. It can be a difficult few minutes, but hang in there. The good news is that you probably won't have to go back to this doctor for a whole year!

2

Taking Care of Business: Your Growing Body and All Its Bits

What do you think of when you think about growing up? Getting your period? Growing breasts? Learning to drive a car? All these things are important parts of growing up, and we'll talk about them in a bit (well, except for the driving the car part; you'll have to go to driver's education for that), but they aren't the only things affected by this wild and wonderful process called puberty. In this chapter, you'll find some information on how to take care of your body's rapidly changing parts, from head to toe.

❄ Starting at the Top: The Hair on Your Head

Hair care can be a little bit complex for girls. Not only are there many choices of hairstyles to choose from, different hair textures also require different care and maintenance routines. However, many of the basics are the same whether your hair is "high style" or "short and simple."

- **Lather. Rinse. Repeat.** As you get further into puberty, you might find that your hair is more oily than it used to be. That's those pesky hormones at work again! If you are very active and have fine or oily hair (or both), you might need to wash your hair every day. If you have coarser, textured hair, you won't need to wash it as frequently, since that would only dry out your hair and scalp. For thick, coarse hair, washing your hair with shampoo once a week might be plenty. Coarser hair might also need a deep conditioning treatment every week.
- **Use hair care products made specifically for your type of hair.** Different hair textures need different grooming products. Check labels or ask for help at the drug store if you're not sure what to buy. The place where you get your hair cut might have suggestions too, but keep in mind that products bought in the hair salon are almost always more expensive than products bought anywhere else.
- **Hair can't take the heat.** Chemical processes (like perms or hair coloring), and processes where you apply a lot of heat to your hair (like blow-drying, curling, and straightening) damage your hair and make it harder to take care of in the long term. The less you use these processes, the fewer special conditioning products you will need.

✿ Ears so Dear

If you ask your doctor or nurse practitioner, they will probably say the most important thing you can do for your ears is not to stick things in them! Pen caps, paper clips, and even cotton-tipped swabs can all really hurt your ears if you stick them in too deep. Washing your hair regularly should keep your ears clean, but it can help to scrub lightly on the external part of your ear (the part that's not a hole in your head) with a washcloth. Make sure you get behind your ears where dirt can easily collect. Although you might not see it, it can be obvious to other people, especially if you have short hair.

You know that wax you have in your ears? You might think it's gross, but it has an important job: it keeps dirt from getting further down into your ear where it can do real damage! So make peace with your earwax and let it do its job. If you feel like your ears are clogged or you're having trouble hearing, have a chat with your health care provider about things you can do to help get rid of some of the wax.

❋ Oh, Eye See

What are those two things in between your ears? Oh, wait, they're your eyes! I'm sure we don't need to tell you how important your eyes are to you; you're probably using them right now to read this book! The main thing to remember with your eyes is that if you are having trouble seeing, you need to tell the adults in your life so you can get your eyes checked. Some people have trouble seeing things that are close to them. These people are farsighted. Most people who have trouble seeing, though, are nearsighted, meaning they can see things that are close to them, but have trouble seeing the blackboard (or smartboard) and other things that are further away.

If you do have trouble seeing, you might need glasses. Lots of people have glasses, and they come in all kinds of fun colors and styles. While they might be difficult to deal with at first, you'll get used to them, and you might even forget you have them on! If you're worried about liking your first pair of glasses, ask your friend to go with you when you go to pick out your frames.

They might give you the confidence to feel like you're picking something awesome and stylish. After you've had glasses for a while, you might look into getting contact lenses. Some girls feel more comfortable about their appearance while wearing contacts, while others find it easier to play sports wearing contacts rather than glasses. Contacts do take a certain amount of care, so talk to your parents (and then an eye doctor) to find out if they are a good option for you.

❀ Facing Your Face

When you're in the midst of puberty, your face can be the focus of a lot of worry and concern because of one word: acne (also known as "pimples" or even "zits").

Almost no one gets through puberty without a few pimples on their face, but knowing that doesn't make it any easier when they start popping up. Pimples happen when excess oil becomes trapped in your pores and combines with bacteria (i.e., germs) and dead skin cells. The extra oil on your skin is thanks to the (yes, you guessed it) hormones in your body. Even if you might not zap your zits away overnight, there are some things you can do to help your skin look and feel better.

- Whether you have acne or not, you should be washing your face once a day. Washing does not mean scrubbing—you're a girl, not a kitchen pot, after all! Use gentle, non-scented soap and warm water, or a specially designed face wash. It's also best to try not to touch your face, because touching your face helps spread germs and can lead to more breakouts.
- If you have more than an occasional pimple problem, you might be tempted to try the many products that promise to chase away the "zit monster." The most common and effective

treatments that you can get without a prescription contain benzoyl peroxide or salicylic acid. You can buy these at the drugstore. Follow the directions carefully and don't use more than the label says; benzoyl peroxide and salicylic acid can be very irritating or even burn your skin if you use too much!

- If the over-the-counter products don't help, talk with your parents about visiting a dermatologist (a doctor who specializes in the treatment of problems of the skin).
- If you do get a pimple, don't pick at it or (and this is very tempting) pop it. This just irritates the skin more and can cause a deeper infection, which can cause a permanent scar.
- Make sure to wear sunscreen and protect your skin when you go outside! A sunburn can irritate and damage your skin, causing even more skin problems.

❊ Keeping Your Teeth from Giving You Grief

By the time you read this book, you're old enough and responsible enough that no one is standing over you making you brush your teeth. The adults in your life probably already trust you to do a good job with this bit of personal hygiene. You probably know quite a bit about how to take care of your teeth, so this is just a quick review of some important oral health facts:

- Look for a toothbrush that has soft bristles. A toothbrush that has hard bristles can actually make tiny abrasions in your gums and lead to more problems!

- Replace your toothbrush every three to four months. The bristles get worn out after that point and can't really get your teeth clean, and bacteria can start to grow between the bristles, so you'll just be sticking germs back into your mouth!
- Don't forget to brush all the surfaces of your teeth: outside (the sides touching your cheeks), inside, and all the flat surfaces. Make sure to brush in small circles to help dislodge any food or plaque stuck on your teeth. You should brush your tongue, too, because bacteria can hide there and lead to very smelly breath!
- Remember, in order to get your teeth really clean, you need to brush them for two to three minutes, which is a longer time than you might think. Using the timer on a microwave or your cell phone can be a good way to find out if you're brushing long enough, or pick a song that is three minutes long and play that while you brush. Don't sing along, though—you might bite yourself!
- Floss, floss, floss! Flossing removes food bits and bacteria from in between your teeth, helps you avoid cavities, and keeps your gums strong. If winding the floss around your fingers is too clumsy for you, you can buy single-use floss picks that are small pieces of plastic with the floss already attached. They are not as cheap, but they make flossing much easier.

✼ Do I Have to Go?: Girls and the Dentist

There is a lot you can do to make your teeth healthier at home, but there are some things (like filling a cavity) that can only be done at the dentist's office. Even though not all families have health insurance and not all health insurance plans cover going to the dentist, there are ways people (especially kids) can still get good dental care. Talk to your school nurse for some ideas about how the adults in your life can make this happen.

Some people (not just kids) don't like going to the dentist. If this is the case for you, make sure you ask questions before you get to the dentist's office. Ask the adult who made the appointment for you why you have the appointment: Are you only having your teeth cleaned, or do you need something more done? Then, when you get to the dentist's office, before you open your mouth and say "ahhh," ask the dental hygienist or the dentist to explain exactly what is going to happen, step-by-step. Some procedures at the dentist's office might be uncomfortable, and the more information you have about when and how things might not feel so good, the more you can prepare yourself. A surprise trip to the movies might be a fun thing, but a surprise in the dentist's chair is anything but fun! We're not saying that having all the information is going to make your trip to the dentist's office like a fun trip to the zoo, but the more information you have, the better prepared you will be for what will happen.

❋ Brace Yourself: The Drama of Braces

Lots of kids (and adults even) have braces. But even though braces are very common, sometimes even hearing that they might have to get braces makes girls sweat.

The most common reasons people need braces are because their teeth are crooked or because their upper and lower jaws are not the same size. Both of these problems can make it harder to care for your teeth. Braces don't just improve your smile; they can make your entire mouth healthier.

Getting braces is a perfect time to start taking more responsibility for your health. Ask your orthodontist (a dentist that specializes in braces) about how you should care for your braces, what kind of foods you should avoid, and what you should do if part of your braces breaks off, gets bent, or irritates the inside of your mouth.

❀ Underarm Thoughts

You may have noticed that you are a little stinkier under your arms than you used to be; or if you haven't noticed, your older brothers and sisters might have decided to inform you. This, again, is all part of the puberty process. Those hormones buzzing around your body can change the way your sweat smells and leave you smelling like a gym sock. Pee-yew! Frequent bathing with very deliberate attention to your armpits can help a lot. You can buy special deodorant soap to use on the particularly smelly parts of your body, but try to use a milder soap on the rest of your body (i.e., your arms and legs), because deodorant soap can be very drying.

You may want to start experimenting with different types and brands of deodorant until you find one that works best with your body chemistry. Deodorant comes in many different forms, including roll-ons, solids, and sprays. Avoid deodorants that are labeled "deodorant/antiperspirant." An antiperspirant will actually stop you from sweating, not just from smelling like B.O. Since sweating is a natural body process that helps us cool off, antiperspirants aren't great for your health, so it's best to stick with deodorant.

❄ OMG Hair!

Growing hair under your arms and on your legs is a part of growing up. For many years (and in most cultures), women didn't remove any of this hair. Of course, women showing their legs or armpits in public made people in some cultures faint as recently as 150 years ago, so hair there was the least of anyone's problems.

However, about 100 years ago, companies that make safety razors (the kind encased in plastic as opposed to just the sharp razor part by itself) realized they would have many more customers if they convinced women that they needed to shave every day. So as fashions started revealing the legs and armpits (now with 90 percent less fainting), the companies that made razors started placing lots of ads in women's magazines which made leg and armpit hair seem like something dirty or ugly. One ad even compared having leg hair to having leprosy, which was a dreaded disease at the time. With that kind of pressure, you can see why the women said, "OK, OK, we'll start shaving everything."

Even though many women shave their legs and armpits, you should know there are no medical or hygienic reasons to shave or remove hair anywhere on your body, and many cultures don't even consider it. Some girls still feel like they would be more comfortable without hair. If that's you, talk with your mom or another adult at home about the best way to get rid of it. One common way to do this is by shaving. If you hair is a coarser texture, shaving might not work as well for you, so you might want to experiment with other ways of removing unwanted hair (like depilatory creams).

A Beginner's Guide to Shaving

While having hair on your legs (and arms and the rest of your body) is completely natural, some girls like to remove it. Here are some tips to help your first shave go a bit smoother (pun intended).

❀ **Hop in the shower.** Don't ever shave dry legs. The heat and moisture from your shower will help your shave go much smoother and help you avoid cuts and nicks.

❀ **Don't feel like you have to spend more on shaving cream aimed at women.** Shaving cream is shaving cream. Using shaving cream does make shaving go easier, though, so try to use it. If you run out of shaving cream, you can use conditioner in a pinch, just make sure the adults in your life pick up more shaving cream next time they're at the store!

❀ **Use a new razor and replace your razor regularly.** Old razors won't cut the hair very well, but they may cut you!

❀ **Start at your ankles and shave up.** This can help you avoid nicking yourself and will make sure you get the closest shave. Most people don't shave past the knee, but if you do decide to shave higher up, make sure to be careful on the back of your legs—a cut back there can really sting!

❀ **Put some lotion or moisturizer on your legs after you are done.** This will keep your skin from getting dry.

❉ Keeping Your Feet Neat

Although you might not think about your feet as body parts that need much care, they do some of the hardest work for you. It's worth taking a look at what they might need to function best and what you can do to help them out.

First of all, feet need good, supportive shoes that fit properly. Especially as you are growing quickly in these fun-filled (ha ha) puberty years, you should be measured with the foot-measuring thing (it's called a Brannock Device, but that makes it sound kind of scary) every time you buy shoes. Did you know it's important to measure both feet? Your feet can grow at different rates, and having a too small shoe can make you pretty sore after a while!

Even though you might be absolutely desperate to wear them, especially as you get older, there are very few types of high heels that provide good support for your feet. High heels can cause blisters, hammertoes, and bunions, not to mention leg and back problems! If high heels are a "must have" in your wardrobe, make sure you get shoes that have some room near the toes. Shoes built with a suitable "toe box" are not as hard on your feet as those that crush your toes into a point. Also, save the high heels for special occasions where you won't have to wear them for more than a few hours at a time, and when you won't have to do too much while you're wearing them. Sitting at a party may be a high-heels occasion, but running for a bus or walking through a museum is definitely not.

A very common foot problem that almost everyone gets sometime in their life is called "athlete's foot."

Athlete's foot is spread in places that are dark and damp and where people go barefoot. Sounds like the locker room where athletes hang out, right? Athlete's foot is a kind of fungus that anyone (not just athletes) can get. You can prevent it by wearing flip-flops or shower shoes in public showering areas—just make sure to keep special ones just for this purpose so they don't have outside germs on them! If you notice itching and peeling on your feet, especially around and in between your toes, you might have athlete's foot. It's easy to treat athlete's foot with antifungal sprays or powders that the adults in your life can buy at a grocery or drug store. Make sure you wash and dry thoroughly between your toes before you put on the antifungal spray, and then wash your hands right away before you touch your face or any other body part. The fungus that causes athlete's foot might like your feet best, but it's happy to live anywhere on your body, including places you definitely don't want fungus hanging out!

Feet are not the sweetest-smelling parts of our bodies, but there are simple and easy things to do to make your feet smell less yucky. Washing your feet is important, of course, but it's also important to always wear socks with your shoes. You'll want to air out your shoes between when you wear them, too. You'll notice some shoes get stinkier than others: shoes that are made out of non-breathable materials like plastic will make your feet sweat more. Make sure you wash your feet every day and dry them well, especially in between your toes.

✻ Loving Your Body Even When It's Hard

Did you know the most important thing you can do for your rapidly changing body is to love it? Every day we are bombarded with images of what a woman should look like from commercials on TV, magazine covers, and billboards, but most of the women in those pictures have spent literal hours getting ready for the picture to be taken. They have teams of people to apply makeup and do their hair, and even after the pictures are taken, anything that doesn't look "perfect" is fixed by manipulating the photo itself. Most of these photos are created to sell products that girls and women buy to look more like the photos! The real purpose of these flawless photos is to make you feel bad about yourself. Fight back and don't let them have that power!

Our bodies are very diverse and wonderful and come in all different shapes and sizes. Comparing your body to someone else's body will never make you happy and will not make you healthy, either. Taking care of your body and loving your body for what it is and what you can do with it, on the other hand, will help you be happier and healthier.

❋ Girls and Food

Girls as young as six or seven sometimes talk about "being fat" or needing to "go on a diet." While it's important to make good food and movement choices so our bodies can run well and we can do things that give us joy, going on a diet is a really bad idea, especially for young girls. Here are just a few reasons why:

- Young girls need good nutrition and calories to keep growing.
- Dieting makes food the enemy. Food is fuel and it should be fun, and learning to make good choices can be part of that fun.
- Dieting is often done to become a specific size or look the "right" way, but bodies come in lots of shapes and sizes. These variations are natural and normal.
- Because a diet usually has a list of "good" and "bad" foods, dieting makes it harder to listen to what your body really wants.

- Most fad diets require that you give up entire categories of food, which makes it very unlikely that your body will get the nutrients it needs.
- Dieting doesn't usually lead to long-term weight loss, and depriving ourselves can make it difficult to have a healthy relationship with food later on.

Learning what to eat is important, but so is learning how to eat. For example:

- Work with your body. Your body sends you signals that say, "I'm hungry," and it's important to be able to know what they feel like. When you are eating because you are upset or bored instead of hungry, it's harder to make healthy food choices.
- Make food choices based on how you feel after you eat certain foods. Do you have more energy? Do you feel tired? Restless? Queasy?
- If you are looking to get away from junk food, try different foods that might especially interest your taste buds, like foods from another culture, or foods that are flavored with different ingredients than you are used to.
- Although fresh fruit is a tasty and convenient snack, sometimes girls get bored with the old "apple in the lunch" routine. See if you can try different kinds of fresh fruit and remember: fruit is best when it is in season (meaning close to the time it was picked). You might have learned this when you tried a supposedly fresh tomato in the middle of the winter only to find it didn't taste much better than cardboard. If your family can afford it, try organic fruit—it has an even better flavor.
- Don't get discouraged if you are trying to eat more healthily and fall back into old patterns. It takes time to change habits.

If you keep listening to your body and keep trying to make choices that will give you energy, you'll find yourself eating well.

❈ Healthy Eating for Girls on the Go

If you've got a busy schedule, it can seem like a lot of work to try to eat healthy food. Here are some tricks that may help guide you to the types of food that will keep you healthy while satisfying your taste buds:

- Always carry a piece of fruit with you. Stick with hard fruits like apples and oranges, since softer ones like pears and bananas will turn into a mushy, soup-like substance in your backpack. In the winter months, there is nothing like the sweet taste of a clementine to wake up your taste buds, and since it comes with its own wrapping (also known as the peel), you can just grab it and go when you are running out the door.

- Think about "healthier" choices instead of "good" or "bad" foods. You can't always get organic kale and steamed chicken breasts for dinner, and even if you could, you'd get bored fast. Instead, when you can't get the healthiest thing, look for food that is less processed and has fewer additives. For example, if you only have access to a vending machine for an after-school snack, you might not be able to get baby carrots, but you could probably find pretzels or another food that's not fried and maybe has some nutritious content.

- Carry nuts in a small bag with you at all times. Nuts last even longer than fruit, are less messy to eat, and have protein so they'll keep you full for a long time!

❀ Better Choices in Fast Food

Fast food is easy, cheap, tasty, and, let's face it, it's everywhere. Since fast food isn't going to disappear anytime soon, you will need to take charge and make your own healthier choices as you get older:

- Again, don't think about "good" and "bad" foods. There are no specific foods that are good or bad, but some foods don't really fuel your body very well. Many fast food choices are in this category.

- Sometimes a salad can be a good fast food choice, but beware of adding lots of dressing or other random bits of non-vegetable-type food. Those don't add much nutrition, but can add a lot of calories. It's like putting a fully loaded hamburger on your salad.

- Fast food is highly processed; in other words, it's been a long time since it looked like the food that someone grew (if it ever was). Plus, because it comes from so far away and has been frozen, canned, or bagged, it takes a lot of preservatives and chemicals to make it taste good. These preservatives and chemicals make it harder for your body to use fast food as fuel.

- When in doubt and there is a fruit option, consider taking the fruit.

- Just because the drink that comes with a fast food meal has the word "juice" in it, that doesn't mean it's healthy. Watch out for sweeteners like high fructose corn syrup, which your body has a very hard time using for fuel.
- Think about training your taste buds. It's true that French fries taste great, and fast food French fries taste especially awesome because they're often sprayed with a sugar solution before they're fried, but apples can taste pretty great if you get in the habit of eating them.
- Make small changes first. If you usually eat an entire fast food meal and drink a large soda, maybe you can start with carrying your own water bottle and eliminating the soda. After you've done that for a while, maybe switch it up from French fries to apples.

❈ Worried About Weight

Even though it's much healthier (and much more fun!) to think in terms of healthy eating and healthy movement choices rather than diets and exercise, girls are under a lot of pressure to be slender and many girls are very afraid of the "F" word: fat.

Television and movies don't do a good job in showing girls the range of healthy body types that are out there. If you only get your body image from the media, you might think that every girl is tall and slender. Not true! Girls come in all different shapes and sizes; the trick is to find and accept the healthiest size and weight for your body type.

If you're worried about your weight, take a minute and think about what you are really scared of. Are you worried that you will be unhealthy? Are you worried that you will never have a boyfriend?

Are you worried that you'll be teased? Ask your parents to help you figure out if what you're worried about is likely to happen and if it does happen, what your options are. You can also talk with a health professional (like a doctor or nurse practitioner) about whether your weight is right for you.

❈ About Eating Disorders

There are two main types of eating disorders. If a girl has anorexia nervosa, she will intentionally starve herself. If she has bulimia, she will eat huge amounts of food and then force herself to get rid of (purge) the food from her system. Both types of eating disorders are very serious conditions and require the girl to get professional help to live a healthy, active, happy life.

Eating disorders typically begin around the time a girl starts puberty and can last her whole life if not treated. Here are some signs to watch for in yourself and your friends. If you think you or someone you know has a problem, talk to an adult you trust.

Anorexia Nervosa:

Girls with anorexia nervosa:
- Are often convinced that they are fat. Although they may be "as thin as a rail" or "a stick figure" to other people, when they look in the mirror they see someone who is overweight.
- May be obsessed with food. They may talk about it constantly and even cook huge meals, but not eat the food themselves.
- Are usually obsessed with exercise. They may work out for hours to get rid of any calories they may have eaten.

Bulimia:

It may be more difficult to tell if a girl has bulimia because she may not be very slender. However, here are some things to watch for.

Girls with bulimia:

- Are very body and weight conscious and are frequently dieting. They think a lot about body weight and shape and use it to raise or lower their self-esteem.
- Eat an excessive amount of food during a short period of time and feel a lack of control over how much they eat. They often feel like they cannot stop eating until all the food is gone.
- May force themselves to vomit or use other methods to prevent weight gain from the large amounts of food they've eaten.

Treatment for bulimia and anorexia nervosa include therapy with a trained psychologist, medication, and sometimes hospitalization. Remember—help is out there, but sometimes the hardest step is asking for it.

❁ Girls and Sports

If you like them, team sports can be a great way to help you keep fit, spend time with friends, and enjoy what your body can do! Team sports can be especially good for girls because they can help you keep your body confidence as you go through puberty. Sports can be a good way to ensure that you still do the things you enjoy, even if you might feel a little bit awkward about the way you move in your always-changing body.

Some reasons to play a team sport:

- Release stress and pent-up energy from sitting still all day. After all, it's hard to worry about your math homework when you're trying to hit a fastball!
- Have fun.

- Get exercise and enjoy what your body can do.
- Learn skills like how to pass and dribble, as well as self-confidence, self-discipline, and teamwork.
- Make friends.

Did you notice what wasn't on the list of benefits of team sports? "Feeling great because you win every game." No one is going to argue that winning isn't fun, especially compared to losing, but if there is too much emphasis placed on winning, sports actually become less fun. If the only thing that makes sports fun is winning, and only one team can win, that means only half the players get to enjoy it! Would you and a bunch of your friends go to a movie you knew half of you would hate? That would be a waste of time. Sports are the same way if the only goal is winning.

Some girls find losing especially hard, if that is true for you, you can set personal goals for each game that don't depend on winning. For example, if you're an outfielder, your goal could be to catch 80 percent of the fly balls that come to you. If you struggle to support your teammates, maybe your goal could be to find five things to compliment other players about.

Sometimes adults push kids too hard in sports. While pushing yourself a little can be good, pushing yourself and your growing body too much can lead to permanent injuries. If you are feeling so much pressure that sports have lost some of their fun for you, it might be time to talk to your parents about this.

❈ Sports Safety

Sports accidents do sometimes happen even if you're very careful, but there are steps you can take to prevent serious or long-lasting injuries. One of the most important things you can do is to wear the right protective gear. Your head is super important since it's where your brain is kept. It's also one of the easiest parts of your body to protect: simply make sure to wear the helmet made for the sport you're playing. Have your coach adjust the helmet for you and always use the chin strap (if the helmet comes with one). Otherwise, your helmet might go flying one way and your head flying the other way at the exact moment when they should be sticking together! You also need to wear a helmet when you're riding your bike; in some places it's even the law that you need to wear your helmet, and the adults who are in charge of you can get into trouble if you ride without one.

Another very important way you can keep from being injured when you play sports is to warm up and stretch out before you start. Warming up and stretching give your muscles a chance to wake up and get the blood flowing so you can perform at your best without getting hurt. There are special areas of your body you'll need to concentrate on stretching for different sports. Your coach should know all about this. If you are playing a sport that doesn't require teams or coaches (running or skateboarding, for example), you'll have to do your own research about stretching out. Someone more experienced in the sport may have some ideas, or you can research online or at your local library.

The final word of advice for staying safe when playing sports: don't play if you are hurt. It's easy to get caught up in the excitement of the final play or a close game. Sometimes things do hurt a little bit when you're pushing yourself physically—that's part of being active! But playing when you actually have an injury can turn something small and not necessarily serious into an injury that can give you problems for a long time. Since you're going to need your body for the rest of your life, it's not worth doing permanent damage! Anyone who asks you to play when you are actually injured is not respecting you or your body.

❈ Get Moving

Little kids naturally move around a lot. However, once kids go to school and have to start sitting still more than six hours a day, they slow down. Often the only time kids get time to jump and run around is at a very short recess. Then, to make it worse, as kids get older, organized sports become a more and more important part of outside play and physical education. Sometimes kids who aren't Joe or Janet Jock stop enjoying moving their bodies and become more sedentary. This is not healthy, and it's definitely not fun.

Even if you're not a basketball superstar, there are lots of ways you can make physical activity a part of your life. You can:

- Try individual sports, or sports that don't require a whole team to participate, like running or tennis.
- Experiment with activities that you might enjoy but aren't competitive. Yoga is a good example. No one loses at yoga!
- Go for walks. There's a whole world out there to explore, even without leaving your neighborhood.
- Go for hikes (hikes are basically walks where there are lots of trees).
- Relearn active games you might remember from when you were younger, like tag or kickball. You might want to stay away from dodgeball, which too often causes hurt feelings or worse!

- Suggest social activities with your friends that involve physical activity. Maybe go for a bike ride together or go in-line skating.
- You could always play the kind of video games that require you to run in place, jump around, or dance.
- Explore ways to get around that involve movement, like running, walking, or riding a skateboard or scooter (with protective equipment, of course).
- Go swimming on a hot day. If you haven't been moving in a while, swimming is an especially good choice because it's easy on your joints!
- Go to the mall. Yes, that's right, the mall. Walking around the mall can be good exercise. Some malls even open early to give walkers a safe place to get moving.

Adding some movement into your day can really help you feel happier and less stressed while going through puberty. You can probably come up with even more fun ways to get your body moving if you think about it. Remember, people come in all different weights, heights, sizes, and shapes. If you develop loving habits and take care of your body now while you're still young, you will be healthier—and much happier—as you grow up. The mind and body connection is a real thing!

✿ Yawn: Girls and Sleep

When you were younger, the adults in your life were more likely to enforce a strict bedtime. Now that you are older, you may still have a bedtime, but getting enough sleep is starting to become more and more your responsibility.

The average girl your age needs 10 hours of sleep a night in order to grow and be healthy, but you might need a little bit more or less sleep than that. If you have trouble waking up in the morning, can't concentrate at school, or fall asleep during class, it might not be because you're bored—you just might not be getting enough sleep.

If you have trouble getting to sleep, one of the things you can do to help yourself is to create a bedtime routine. If you do the same things every night, it will help your body recognize, "Hey, it's time for sleeping now!" A bedtime routine might look something like this: get in your pajamas, brush your teeth, say goodnight to your parents, read for 15 minutes, and then turn out the lights on another great day.

One of the most important things you can do to fall asleep quicker and sleep better is to put away the screens! Looking at the kind of light that comes from tablets or smartphones actually tells your brain to be awake. It can be fun to huddle under the covers texting your best friends until late at night, but when those late nights turn into cranky mornings, it might not be worth it.

❈ 3 ❈

Feelings and Friends

❈ Being the Boss of You

With your body and what seems like your whole life changing more every day, it can be easy to get overwhelmed with very strong feelings. It's really important to remember that feelings are not right or wrong: they just are. For example, it's not bad to feel angry about something. The fact that you are feeling angry tells you something about the situation or yourself. It might mean you need to work on changing the situation (if you can), or you might need to work on how you view the situation if you don't want to continue to feel angry. The problem with strong feelings only comes when we act on the feelings in a way that hurts ourselves or others.

Here's an example: if your little brother "borrows" your toothbrush to spread the glue on his model cars, it would be very normal to feel angry. In the moment, you might want to use his toothbrush to clean the bathroom floor. But you can probably see why talking to an adult about the problem might work out better for everyone involved.

Of course, in order to make the better decision when you have strong feelings, you need a way to get rid of some of the big physical and emotional energy that comes from them. That way you'll be able to respond instead of just reacting.

A common way for girls to work out strong feelings is to talk to a friend. Did you know you can help your friends be better listeners by communicating what kind of support you need from them? For example, if you want your friend to be really paying attention to what you're saying but she seems distracted, try saying, "I have something that I really want to talk to you about. Would you mind if we put down our phones for now and just really talked?" Or if you have a friend who always gives advice when you would rather they just listen, you can say, "I really appreciate that you want to help me out, but right now I really just need to vent." And if you do want advice, you can always ask directly!

You can also write out your feelings. Whether it's a notebook stuck under your mattress, a password-protected file on your computer, or a special leather-bound book with a padlock built in (yes, they do make those), a journal can be a great way to express yourself. Not only can journaling take an edge off some of your strongest feelings and help you calm down before making a decision, it's an awesome tool because you can go back and read over what you've been through in the past and see how you've grown.

Physical activity is also a great way to work out your feelings. A fast walk can not only get you out of the situation for a few minutes, but you might also feel a lot better when you come back! And if you can get someone to walk with you and listen to your feelings, you'll be sure to boost your mood.

❈ Making Friends

As if it isn't enough that your body and your feelings are changing, many girls find this is an age where they have to make a whole new group of friends!

Sometimes this happens because you are going to a bigger middle school and the kids you used to hang out with are in different classes and have a different schedule than you. Sometimes the crowd that you hung out with when you were younger starts doing things you don't like and you need to find a new crowd to hang out with. Sometimes you just find that your interests have changed and you don't have anything in common with your old friends anymore.

Whatever the reason, making new friends can be scary but ultimately rewarding.

It really is a supportive group of friends that will help you get through middle school and—let's be real here—life. This is the time in your life when your family stops being the focus of your social world and your friends fulfill that role, so this is also the moment you can start building excellent friend habits, like making

sure the people you hang out with have the same kind of values as you do. That means that you and your friends think the same things are important.

If you are having trouble finding and keeping good friends, you might try making a list of the qualities (for example, sense of humor, likes to do the same things, even-tempered) that you are looking for in a friend. Look around to see who has those qualities— it might even be someone you weren't expecting!

Some friendships just happen, but more often you need to make a special effort to find good friends. Being friendly (waving to people, smiling, cracking jokes with them) is a good beginning. Be interested in your new potential friend. Ask them questions about their likes and dislikes, how things are going for them, or what kinds of things they like to do after school.

One way of really cementing a friendship is by doing things together besides watching TV. Activities that don't require you to interact much can't help you get to know your friend very well— try going to the park, playing a board game, or building something together instead!

If you want to change crowds, you can sometimes start by making a few new friends. Eat lunch with someone new, or chat with them between classes. You can find things you have in common this way.

❉ Friendship Skills

Although in some ways it's natural to be a good friend to someone you care about, there are skills that can make being a good friend easier.

For example, everyone makes mistakes in friendships: we say something that we don't mean when we are tired or angry, or we let our good-natured teasing go too far. One of the surest ways to keep a friendship growing strong is to apologize when you do something to hurt your friend's feelings. It works best if you don't say, "I'm sorry but..." and then go on to explain to the person why they are wrong. That's not really an apology; it's a way of keeping an argument going!

Another thing that helps keep a friendship growing is talking through disagreements before they get really big. If a friend borrows your sweater and doesn't bring it back when she promised to, it's better to mention it the first time she does it and not wait until the 10th time and blow up. She might not even know that it bothers you until you tell her.

Another important building block of friendship is being a good listener about big and small things. When your friend has a problem, most of the time they won't need you to give them advice and won't need you to come up with a solution. They probably just need you to really sit still and listen to what they have to say. Sometimes this isn't easy; your friend might want to talk about a movie that you thought was stupid. Interrupting with "booooorrring" might make your friend laugh the first time, but it won't feel great when they do it back to you. If you make the extra effort to pay attention to what your friend has to say, you might become more interested in the conversation and decide the movie wasn't stupid after all!

When friends are going through hard times, you can help by offering to assist them with tasks that might be overwhelming for them. You might have to help them figure out what you could do that would be helpful. For example, if your friend breaks their arm and has to spend a few days in the hospital, you could offer something like, "I could help you by going and picking up your homework at school, or I could bring you some magazines to read.

Does one of those sound like something that would make this day better?"

Just as your friends should expect you to be there for them during stressful times, you can expect the same things from your friends. If you need help, call them. If they need help, be there. Together you will make it through all the challenging times that growing up can dish out.

✽ Is a Crush a Must?

Sometimes people pressure girls in puberty to start looking at boys a little differently or suggesting that the way they interact with boys must change. At this point in your life you may have started to crush on boys, or you might be completely uninterested in any kind of romance.

This is a time in your life when you are exploring relationships and getting to know yourself better. Don't put pressure on yourself to start the dating part of your life too soon. If you are interested in dating or "going out with" someone, work on being friends first. Try different fun activities where you can get to know that person. Going to the movies (a very typical first date), doesn't allow for much talking, so it might not be the best way to get to know someone. In fact, there will be less pressure for both of you if you go out with a few other friends (they can be on a date or not) for a group activity, instead of hanging out one-on-one.

If you feel a lot of pressure from your friends to jump into dating before you are ready, it can help to make at least a few friends who are running at your same speed when it comes to romantic relationships.

The good news is whether you feel interested or ready for dating or not, all the friendship skills you are building in these years will help you when you are ready.

✿ A Few More Tips About Body Language and Listening

When you're talking with anyone (a friend or a teacher or a parent or another adult), it's important to show that you are listening and that you are not just waiting for your turn to talk. It can be helpful to wait a few moments after the other person stops speaking before you start. This can be really hard sometimes if you are excited about the conversation or nervous.

Another great way to move the conversation along is to ask questions. This might come naturally when trying to understand the story, but you can also say things like, "Really, wow, what happened next?" or, "So what did you say then?" or, "And what did the next text say?"

Try to avoid bored-sounding responses like, "Uh huh" or, "Mmmmm," which make it seem like you are thinking about something else, even if you aren't! Part of being a good listener is learning to read body language. You probably already do this a lot of the time! If a friend has balled-up hands and a very red face but says, "I'm OK," you might notice that their words and actions aren't matching up and should ask them another question or try to comfort them.

Your body language matters too! If you are squirming or looking away or messing around on your phone while your friend, teacher, or family member is talking, it looks like you are not interested in what they have to say. Crossing your arms in front of you can make it look like you are not open to what they are talking about, or even that you are mad!

Instead, lean toward the person a tiny bit while they're talking and make eye contact as they speak. You don't want to actually stare at the person—that can seem creepy. Just look into their eyes naturally so they know you are listening.

❖ Personal Empowerment

A girl's life can feel like a roller coaster when she's smack-dab in the middle of puberty. One minute you might feel super happy, but the next moment you might feel extra sad. Add this to all the changes your body is going through and the fact that you're trying to figure out how to build middle school friendships, and it's a lot of difficulties to handle all at once.

A healthy (or even growing) dose of personal empowerment during these years can help your days go smoother, even if they aren't always easy. Personal empowerment is a pretty simple concept; it just means having a feeling or sense of your own power.

If you have a sense of your own power, you will still have the same problems. You'll have pimples you can't control, your friends may turn out not to be friends, and sometimes your basketball team will lose.

But when you have a sense of your own power:

• You understand that you have control over some things in your life.

- You are able to make changes when there are changes to be made, so that you can jump over obstacles or maybe kick them over.
- When you can't change a situation, you find ways of dealing with the reality that you have to live with and don't blame yourself or other people for life not always being perfect.

The adults in your life have hopefully been working with you since you were an infant to develop a sense of personal empowerment. Here are some things you can do to develop this valuable force on your own:

- Read books (fiction is good, but nonfiction is even better) about girls like you who overcame difficulties and then went on to accomplish great things. Pay close attention to what kind of help they had, how they used the resources they had access to, and what they did when they got discouraged.
- Keep your friends who like all of you (your personality and who you are in the world) very close to you and make sure they know how much you appreciate having them around!
- Spend less time with friends who put you down. There's one of these in every crowd: a girl (or guy or adult) who always has to be the star and who complicates everyone's lives by always knowing how everyone should be acting at every single moment and then getting mad when the world doesn't cooperate with them. This person can often be charming and fun when you first

start being friends, but then you will start to notice anytime you have a disagreement they always talk you into taking the blame!

- Learn how to ask for help. As one principal used to say, "Closed mouths don't get fed." No girl can do everything by herself, and what's the fun of that anyway?

- Find activities that stretch you just enough. Sometimes it's easier to be a girl who only takes the classes she knows she can get an A in, or who only plays the one sport she has been playing her whole life. But if you don't reach for something just a bit more difficult, you won't grow.

- Ask the adults in your life for help figuring out how the hard things in your life can help challenge you or help you grow in a positive way. There is a saying, "Whatever doesn't kill you makes you stronger," and that does seem like a bit of an exaggeration. Some hard stuff that doesn't really cause you any physical harm (like parents getting divorced) might just make you more tired and sad, not really stronger. But some challenges in your life can inspire you to dig deeper and find more enthusiasm or energy.

Consent and Boundaries

As more of your life takes place when others aren't watching, you have to develop your own ethics and boundaries.

One area you need to be really clear about is only touching people when they want to be touched. Your body belongs to you and people should not touch it without your OK, also called your consent. In the same way, other people's bodies (including kids of all ages) are theirs, and you shouldn't touch them without their consent. This includes touching that you think is a joke like holding someone down and tickling them.

It's really important to respect physical boundaries, but it's just as important to respect other people's privacy, which is another form of boundaries.

Don't look through someone else's phone or things if they haven't given you permission, or push them to talk about things or answer questions they don't want to answer.

You can think of another person's body, personal space, belongings, and private thoughts like their own little house they carry around all the time. Just like you wouldn't barge into someone's house without knocking and asking to be let in, you should ask and then wait for permission before you go inside their boundary house.

What Do These People Want from Me?: Life at Home

You might have noticed this book sometimes talks about the "adults in your life," "adults at home," or "guardians," as well as using the more specific term "parents." That's because not all girls are raised by their parents. Some girls are raised by a single parent, grandparents, two moms, two dads, in foster families, blended families, by aunts and uncles, or combinations of the above. We want those girls to understand that this book is for them, too. Every family is unique and different from every other family. What's important is that you have an adult in your life whom you can trust.

❋ Changing You, Changing Home

Many girls, no matter what their family situation, say that as they enter their late preteen years, life at home gets a whole lot more, well, "interesting" is one way to say it! It's natural for your friends to become more important to you as you get older, this is an important part of growing up. At the same time, figuring out how to still get along with your family even though things are changing is a very important skill. Remember: you can make a difference in your life at home!

✿ My Mom Is Driving Me Crazy!

You may have noticed that as you've gotten closer to puberty, you have more conflict with the adults in your life, whether they are foster parents, grandparents, or your aunt. Sometimes this conflict is around certain issues, like after-school activities, curfews, schoolwork, video games, or watching TV. Sometimes it might seem like the conflict comes out of nowhere and you find that your parents can annoy you just by walking into the room! This isn't fun, but it is normal. The job of kids as they get older is to separate from their parents until they are independent enough to live on their own. The job of parents is to give kids loving guidance, set limits, and make sure they are actually ready to live on their own when the time comes.

So while kids and parents mostly have the same goal (for the kid to be ready to be an adult when the time comes), kids and adults don't always agree about how to get to this goal. That's where the conflict comes in. No matter how unreasonable your parents, or guardians' actions might seem to you (and, of course, some adults are more reasonable than others), you can't control them. You can control your own actions, though, and sometimes this can help make things a little smoother around the house. Here are some tips for maintaining a good relationship with the adults in your life:

- **Keep talking.** If you explain something once and your parents look at you like you're an alien dropped from a spaceship into their living room, it's easy to clam up, give up, and go to your room, but try giving your parents another chance. Explain again what you're feeling and what you want from them using different words. Ask what part they did understand and start from there. Your parents may never "get" everything about you, but if you give up sharing too early, you might miss the support they do have to offer.

- **Keep listening.** Many families have a "no slammed doors" rule, and when you refuse to listen to anything your parents are saying because you don't agree, it's just like slamming a door. Even if the conversation continues verbally, you don't come any closer to an agreement.

- **Remember, it's not just words that can hurt feelings.** Ever had a friend frown at you when you first arrived at school in the morning? It hurts, doesn't it? If you continually roll your eyes, make a face, or frown at the adults in your life, they are going to have a reaction and you are probably not going to like it.

- **Learn how to "fight fair."** Girls are going to have conflict with parents, (there is simply no way around that), but some conflict can be positive if tempers are kept under control and certain guidelines are observed. For example, avoid name-calling. If you're in the middle of a discussion that is turning into an argument, ask to take a break and calm down, and don't be afraid to apologize if you hurt someone's feelings.

- **Pick your battles.** You don't care about everything equally, so try to give in without a big discussion on some things you care less about. Your parents will listen more closely when you bring up an issue if they don't feel like you are always complaining about every rule they make.

❋ Negotiation: "Please!" Is Not Enough

In order to successfully negotiate with the folks who are the "boss of you" at home, it helps to have some basic understanding of what they want and need.

For example, one of the most common areas of conflict is curfew. You think you're old enough to stay out really, really late, but the adults in your life want you back in the house as soon as the sun goes down.

Despite what it might feel like sometimes, most parents don't set a curfew based on what they think will make you the most miserable or will most effectively ruin your entire social life; they probably have concerns either about your safety or about you getting enough sleep for the next day's activities. It's important to ask what their specific concern is and listen to their answer.

For your negotiation with them to be successful, you'll have to address their concerns. For example, if your parents know that you are at a safe, supervised, age-appropriate activity, they are likely going to be much more flexible about your curfew. Sharing more information about what you are doing and where you are going—even if you think it's boring to talk about these things with your parents—might calm their fears a bit. Brainstorm ways to communicate with them about what's going on and reassure them that you are safe, and try to be open to ideas that they suggest so you can find a way to work together to get to your common goals.

Parents will be more likely to be flexible about curfews if you show them that you have good judgment and a good plan.

For example, talk with them about what you would do if you were at a party and realized there was drinking going on, or your ride home disappeared. Show them how seriously you take your responsibilities and your part of the agreement. For example, the first time you are out after you have agreed on a later curfew, come in ten minutes before you are required to be in.

A final note about negotiation: don't ask for exceptions to rules at the last minute or in front of your friends. A private conversation is going to go better in most cases, because your parents won't feel pressured by the audience.

❁ Chores

Most families have expectations about how kids help out. This might include small things like clearing the table after dinner, or bigger things like housecleaning, or even helping with a family farm or store. These expectations can be a source of conflict between girls and the adults in their lives, especially if girls feel like helping around the house cuts into their social time too much.

Luckily, there are some ways to negotiate about chores so that everyone will feel like they are getting some of their needs met.

If you and your parents or guardians are feeling frustrated around the subject of chores, ask for a family meeting to discuss things. Prepare for the meeting beforehand by thinking about what areas need to change and what compromises seem reasonable to you.

It might help to come armed with some additional chores that you might be willing to do to help the house run smoothly in exchange for having fewer responsibilities in another area. For example, if helping with dinner puts too much pressure on you to get home quickly after sports practice, maybe you could ask what you could help with in the morning instead.

If the adults in your life complain that you are not doing a good job with your chores, ask for more details about exactly what they expect to be done. Try making an actual list by breaking the chore down to its smallest parts and checking each of them off as you do them.

❋ Oh Brother (or Sister): The Art of Being Friends With Siblings

Siblings can be absolutely infuriating! You may get angry if they take something that is yours, go into your room without asking, or bother you when you have friends over. Your older brothers or sisters may try to boss you around and tell you what to do, and your younger brothers or sisters may borrow your things or want to be around you all the time when you just need a break and want to be left alone.

One of the most difficult things about sibling arguments is that they happen in a closed space. When you argue with your friends, you can go home and get away from them, but when you argue with a brother or sister, they are in your house and you may feel like you can never get away from them!

Here are some ways to make and keep sibling peace:

• Go for a walk or go to separate rooms in the house before you lose your temper in an argument.

- If the same argument keeps happening, talk to your parents about what is bothering you. They will most likely be able to give you some advice.
- Set up your own personal space. Even if you share a bedroom, set aside a little place (even in a corner of your bedroom) that is all yours. Make sure you respect your brother or sister's personal space, too, whether it is their room or a part of your shared bedroom. If you do this, they will be more likely to show you the same courtesy.
- Don't do things that break down your relationship with your sisters and brothers. This includes physical violence (hitting, throwing things) but also name-calling, breaking promises, telling secrets, and not respecting property and personal boundaries.
- Work to build your relationship with your siblings. Try and think of shared projects you can do together that will make happy memories, like working together on a scrapbook of your family vacation, or cleaning out the basement to make a cool, new hang-out spot.

❋ 5 ❋

Your Changing Body
in the Outside World
and at School

Do you remember your first day of kindergarten? You might have been worried about not being able to get to the bathroom in time, missing home a lot, or not having much success with scissors. Now that you've successfully dealt with all those challenges, it might be just the tiniest bit frustrating to find that each year in school brings with it new and improved things to worry about!

Most kids—even the very best students for whom schoolwork comes really easily—worry about grades sometimes. You've probably had to adjust your thinking about grades as you've gotten older, since this is just about the time many schools change from the satisfactory or not satisfactory way of grading to giving actual letter (A, B, C, D) grades. It might seem like the whole concept of grades is an evil plan to give adults and kids one more thing to fight about, but grades are really supposed to measure how much you've learned. That's one big reason why the adults in your life want you to earn good grades: they want to know that you are learning something at school. But grades are only one way to measure how much you've learned, and they aren't perfect.

Grades only reflect a certain kind of learning, so if you are a girl who struggles with schoolwork, or has to work really hard to get the kind of grades other students seem to get easily, it does not mean you are not smart. Struggling with schoolwork does not make anyone "dumb," and don't let anyone tell you that it does. If school is not that easy for you, you can bet that you have special skills somewhere else, even if you haven't discovered them yet.

It's true that school life for girls in the older elementary grades or middle school can be difficult in some ways, but exciting things are happening, too. You probably have a little bit more freedom, like being able to choose a few of your classes or even teachers. You might have more fun classes that give you opportunities to do things like learn to play an instrument. Plus, you might have new chances to hang out with other students, learn things together, develop some of your talents, and even find some new talents you didn't even know you had!

✿ Studying: It's a Skill

Although some girls are naturally better students than others, all girls can improve their work in school by having good study habits. The skills you need to be a good student are called (not surprisingly) "study skills," and there are entire books, classes, and websites designed to teach kids how to develop them. But even without reading an entire book, there are some simple steps you can take to improve the way you study:

- The most important study skill is to know what you're supposed to be studying. That's why a small assignment notebook or calendar is something that can be really helpful. Maybe writing down all the assignments you've been given and then crossing them off when you're done doesn't exactly sound like rocket science, but using a "to do" list lets you use your brainpower to do the algebra problems, instead of trying to remember which ones you are supposed to do!

- One way to prepare for class is to engage your brain even before the class starts. As you are getting out your work, or walking into the room, coax yourself to think about the subject you're about to study. You might be thinking, "Ugh, it's bad enough to think about math while math class is going on!"
Still, if you are mentally prepared for what's ahead, you'll be able to follow along right away instead of missing important information while you are switching gears.

- Be an active listener. While the teacher talks, think about how the information fits in with what you've already learned, or how it could be used in your daily life. In some classes, you might need to take notes; this can be a great way to keep your mind on track!

- If you are having trouble concentrating on your studies, use a timer (you can use a cooking timer or the clock on the microwave) to help you develop your "stick-to-it" skills. Hate spelling? Promise yourself to do nothing but study your spelling words for 25 minutes, then set the timer. When you've finished studying, reward yourself with some downtime or a favorite TV show.

- Take extra care to get enough sleep and eat breakfast during the school week. If there are difficulties at home that make it hard for you to do these things, talk with your parents about the situation, or mention it to your teacher or guidance counselor.

- Develop a study routine, like a certain place you always study where you have all the materials you need (extra paper, pens, etc.). Unless you really must use the computer for the assignment, choose a spot far away from the internet. Watching one more YouTube video of someone who taught their dog how to use a yo-yo is always going to seem more interesting than algebra.

- Don't make schoolwork more stressful by putting it off until the last possible minute. A lot of times we procrastinate because a task seems overwhelming. If this is true for you, try to break the assignment into smaller parts and then work on one part at a time.

- If you find you are always checking certain websites "just one more time" before you begin your schoolwork, consider using a browser extension that blocks your online access to those sites for a certain period of time. This will allow your brain to stop thinking about checking in and start thinking about your upcoming history exam.

✿ Getting the Help You Need: Learning Disabilities

Some girls learn better by reading information from a book, some girls learn better by doing an experiment, and other girls might find it easier to understand information that they hear in a song or a podcast.

While all girls learn in their own unique way, some girls experience specific challenges in learning called learning disabilities. A learning disability makes it more challenging for the brain to work with information. Having a learning disability doesn't mean you're not smart—it just means you might need special types of assistance to learn. You might need medication to help with some of the symptoms of your learning disability, extra time to take tests, or a specially trained teacher who can help you figure out the best strategies for you.

Certain learning disabilities can also impact the way you talk and play with other kids because you might have trouble understanding what they mean. For example, some girls might not be able to tell when other kids are joking and when they are being serious.

There are many ways schools and families can support girls with learning disabilities. Each child with a learning disability should have something called an Individual Education Program (IEP), which describes the kind of support and help she gets at school. An IEP is when all the people involved in helping the girl learn sit down together and figure out the best plan. If you are diagnosed with a learning disability, you can contribute to the writing of your IEP. You will need to talk to the adults about how learning is hard for you and what makes it easier. It might not be easy if you are just getting comfortable with the idea of having a learning disability, but learning to advocate for yourself (that is, how to fight for what you need) is a valuable skill for any girl to develop!

If you have a learning disability that makes some types of schoolwork hard for you, it's important to remember all the other things you do well. A girl who might take a really long time to finish a math test might read more quickly than everyone in her grade, while a girl who has trouble chatting casually with her classmates might be able to complete projects quickly or learn chemistry with what seems like no effort at all!

Sometimes adults or other kids will be curious about the special classes you have. Just because someone asks you a question doesn't mean you have to answer it. Aside from people who need to know (your teachers) or people you might want to know (like a supportive friend or two), you don't have to tell anyone how your brain works. If you'd like to explain your learning disability to people who can help advocate for you, ask one of your IEP teachers to help you write a short explanation. You don't have to share it, but at least you will have it handy in case you need it.

✳ Getting Along with Teachers

Some teachers you will meet during your school career will be amazing. You might feel like they care about you, or feel like they really "get" you. That kind of situation usually makes learning easier, even if it isn't always fun.

On the other hand, sooner or later you are going to run into a teacher whom you have a harder time with. It might feel like the

teacher doesn't like you, doesn't understand you, or is too strict. While it's normal to have some teachers you like and some you don't, if your relationship with your teacher is making it hard for you to learn, there are some things you can do to improve the situation.

Since you can only change your own behavior, it's best to look at that first. Do you show up on time? Do you do your homework? Are you respectful? Do you ask questions when you don't understand something? If you answered no to any of these questions, try changing your own behavior first.

If your teacher has some "pet peeves" (behaviors that particularly annoy or bother them), getting along might be as simple as not doing those things! But if you need to bring up an issue with a teacher, do it after class. Most teachers are more relaxed one-on-one than when they are dealing with a whole classroom of kids.

Sometimes it might feel like the problem is the teacher, when the real difficulty is that the subject they teach is one you don't like or that you have a hard time with. If the class is hard for you, make sure the teacher knows you are doing your best. Talk to your parents or other adults at home about the problem. They can help you set up a meeting with the teacher where you can find solutions.

Finally, in a situation like this, it's important to understand that even if you don't connect easily with your teacher, it is not necessarily someone's fault. You are going to like some teachers better than other teachers, just like you like some people better than others. It might not be fun, but you can learn valuable skills about getting along once you learn that you don't have to actually like a teacher to learn from them.

❁ It's Not Just About the Books: Extracurricular Activities and You

In general, the older you get, the more types of organized after-and-before school activities there are for you to get involved in. These activities might be offered through school, through a community organization like a local recreation center, library, or through your house of faith (church, synagogue, or mosque). These activities can be great opportunities to learn new things, practice skills, meet new kids, and learn how to work as a group.

It's important to remember that even though you are still a kid (or between a kid and an adult), your time is precious. If you are involved with an optional activity, it should be because you are enjoying it. Of course, any activity you're involved in is going to have some aspects that aren't that much fun. No one expects you to be jumping up and down in excitement about running laps to get ready for basketball season, and you might prefer not to attend all those extra practices that the chorus has when it gets close to the time for the winter concert, but if you don't get any joy out of being on the basketball team or hate everything about being in the chorus, you might want to consider dropping it.

Here are some tips to make your extracurricular activities extra special:

- Don't take things too seriously. Involvement in outside organized activities can be a really great way to develop self-discipline and learn how to do your best, even when you don't feel like it. However, if you are too intensely focused on achievement and winning instead of just having fun, you miss a lot of the experience. There are plenty of places where life puts pressure on you—don't add to it!

- Honor your schoolwork. Teachers say that after-school jobs can contribute to kids getting lower grades and being super tired in school. If you really want to work as you get older, it's best for your schoolwork to pick jobs where you can decide when to work (like babysitting) or to work very limited hours, like on the weekends or only one or two evenings a week.

- Mix it up. Involve yourself in some activities that are physically active, and some that require more brainpower than muscle power. This is the time to be trying lots of different activities, so you can find out what you like.

- Use extracurricular activities to explore career choices, but don't be in a rush to decide. If you think you want to be a doctor or a nurse, it might be great for you to volunteer at your local hospital when you get old enough. The real-life experience might be enough to tell you, "Wow, this is exactly what I love," or, "Man, I really can't stand the smell of hospitals one bit!" At the same time, just because you couldn't handle hospital smells at 13, it doesn't mean you won't be fine with them by the time you go to college. You have plenty of time to grow and explore!

- When looking for activities to try, think outside the popularity box. You don't have to be good at sports and cheerleading to make good friends. Try joining activities that appeal to you.
- Build some "downtime" in your life. Just hanging out with your friends is an important part of growing up. Everyone—adolescents especially—needs time to be relaxed without the pressure of some structured activity.

Non-Sports Activities

Don't like sports? No problem! Try:

* Writing for the school paper.
* Taking pictures for the yearbook.
* Playing chess on the school chess team or chess club.
* Singing in the choir.
* Acting in (or making sets or costumes for) the school play.
* Running for student government.
* Helping plan dances or other fun events (many schools have a social committee for things like this).
* Learning about running and fixing electronic equipment in the AV club.
* Learning about another culture and language in (for example) a Spanish club.
* Performing a stand-up comedy routine in the school talent show.
* Playing a musical instrument.
* Volunteering as a tutor to someone who needs help.
* Working behind-the-scenes for a sports team keeping score or helping the coach.

❋ 6 ❋

Staying Safe IRL and Beyond

Throughout this book, we've mentioned that every girl has social changes that go along with the physical changes of puberty. This is the time when girls become more involved with their friends and less involved with their parents and family. It might feel strange to be less connected with a parent or grandparent, but as you get older, you will most likely find ways to have relationships with them that reflect the adult you are becoming instead of the kid you used to be.

❋ Interactions with Adults

You might not feel as close to the adults at home as you once did, and that's normal, but try not to shut them out emotionally. Maybe your mom won't be the first person you talk to about a smaller problem at school, but you can still share some of your day with her. These daily interactions will be the building blocks for when you need more serious support, and for your future adult friendship.

Even though you are separating from your primary adult caretakers, this doesn't mean that you need adults in your life any less. In fact, it's even more important now that you have solid, dependable adults around who can support you.

How do you find adults who are not only safe for you to spend time with but who can also support you in a way that will help you grow and push you to be your best? Most of these folks will come in to your life in a natural way: a teacher, a relative, a coach, or someone who works at your house of faith (church, synagogue, or mosque). You might also connect with the parent of a friend, an aunt or a grandparent, or with a mentor who is high school or college-aged. There are also youth mentoring programs in many areas that connect well-screened adults with kids who want  mentoring, specific kinds of support, or who are interested in a particular career. If this sounds like something you'd like, ask your guidance counselor at school about programs that might be available in your local area.

When you're building a friendship with an adult, there might be different rules about communication than there would be with your friends. Many adults don't like to be connected with the young people they work with on social media, or your teachers might only accept friend requests from former—not current—students. This is just to protect your privacy and the privacy of the adult; it's almost never anything personal. Also, adults may or may not want to text with you about plans and to exchange information. Depending (to some extent) on the adult's age and (to a much greater extent) their familiarity with technology, you might not be able to use the latest emojis or text abbreviations. And make sure you use the title you would in person (e.g., Mrs. or Dr.) when you text or email.

When building relationships with the adults in your life, you will need to be thoughtful about your own personal safety. This is a very, very, very important point to remember: it's not the position of the adult (teacher, priest) or their relationship to you (aunt, parent of a friend) that makes them safe for you to spend time with; kids are sometimes hurt by the very people that should be protecting them. What makes an adult safe is that they always respect your boundaries.

Adults who help you at school or in extracurricular activities or are in your family shouldn't ask you to keep secrets about your friendship with them, and your friendship with an adult should feel different than one you have with people your own age.

Hopefully you have been told many, many times by now that your body is your own, and no one has the right to touch you in a way that makes you feel confused, sad, uncomfortable, or scared. No one, except for sometimes a doctor in a doctor's office, should touch you anywhere in your private areas (the areas usually covered by a bathing suit). Even if that person is someone your family knows, a relative, or someone who is very nice to you or pays special attention to you, they still don't have the right to touch you in these areas. If someone does try to touch you in a way that doesn't feel right to you, it's not your fault. It's never your fault when an adult doesn't respect your private areas, even if they say it is. If this happens to you, you need to tell your parents or another adult you trust as soon as possible.

❀ Cliques and Mean Girls

Does it seem like you just woke up one morning to suddenly find a group called "the popular kids" that never existed before? The end of elementary school and the beginning of middle school is about the time when groups of kids often start breaking off into cliques.

Some "grouping off" is to be expected at this age, as girls band together with other kids that have similar interests. A group of friends that travels as a pack because the kids in the group have things they like to do in common (like collect comic books or skateboard) might not really be a true clique. The thing that makes cliques dangerous is when some kids in a clique refuse to allow other kids to be a part of an activity, especially if there is bullying and teasing involved.

It is a rare girl who can make it through to high school without suffering some hard days because of bullying and teasing. A very important thing to remember is that when cliques exist only to keep certain girls out, they are not about socializing and friendship anymore; they are about power and control. Everyone feels insecure at your age, and the kids who run the meanest cliques are usually the kids who feel the most insecure and are trying to make themselves feel better by keeping other kids down.

Not that knowing this really helps, right? Especially when adults give you advice like, "Just ignore it, they will stop teasing you if they see it doesn't bother you," which might be true (maybe, eventually) but is really hard to do when you are stuck at the bus stop for 20 minutes with someone who just made up 13 different rhyming ways to insult you.

The cruelty of girls to one another is something that scientists have gotten involved in studying (really, it's true). They have figured out two things that help protect girls from the effects of being teased: not blaming themselves for what they are being teased about, and having a supportive group of friends.

✿ Peer Pressure

Part of what makes bullying and the "mean girls" so effective is how powerful peer pressure can be. Pressure from peers doesn't always look like the typical scene from a corny movie made by adults where kids sit around in a circle and tell each other, "C'mon, everyone is doing it." Peer pressure can be very subtle. A lot of decisions you make every day might be influenced by information you get from your peers and things you see them do. For example, think about how you made the decision to put on the clothes you have on right now. Hopefully wanting to be comfortable was a part of your decision, but there were probably lots of other thoughts, too—including what your friends would think!

This is why adults are always reminding you how important it is to choose your friends very carefully. The way your friends act, talk, dress, study (or don't study) all have the potential to influence the way you act, talk, dress, and, well, you get the picture.

So obviously, choosing your "peers" carefully is the first step in making sure peer pressure isn't a negative thing in your life. There are also other steps you can take to help push back against peer pressure, for example:

- Practice saying "no" when it isn't super important. This will help you be thought of as someone who doesn't just go along with the crowd. Often kids will stop pressuring you if they know you aren't going to give in, because it makes them look silly.
- If you are anticipating a situation in which you might be under a lot of peer pressure to do something you don't want to do,

brainstorm ways you can deal with it. You might even want to ask someone to role-play with you to get some practice!

- Try not to get caught alone. If you know it's hard for you to say "no" to cutting class with a bunch of other students from your grade, talk with another friend who might be feeling pressure about this. Agree to be each other's peer pressure buddy (you can probably think of a cooler way to say it) to help resist the temptation.

- You don't have to give a detailed answer for every decision you make. Sometimes just saying, "No thanks," and nothing more, can be a powerful way of communicating that the conversation is over. Remember: "no" is a complete sentence!

- If you are having trouble saying "no," remind yourself what you are saying "yes" to. For example, saying no to a cigarette is saying yes to fresh breath and healthy lungs.

- The biggest thing that can help you deal with peer pressure is feeling confident in yourself and in your abilities. As you get involved and find things you are good at, you will feel more able to resist the pressure because you know more about who you are and what you want in life.

- Finally, remember even adults have peer pressure, so while learning how to manage it now might be hard, it will pay off big in the future.

❊ Bullying and Teasing: How to Protect Yourself

Sometimes cliques and mean girls go beyond just being annoying and their behavior becomes straight-up bullying. You are being bullied if other kids at school are saying and doing things that make you feel unsafe, either emotionally or physically.

Bullying can take many forms: it can be someone sending you mean text messages, it can be someone threatening to beat you up, or it can even be some so-called friends asking you to do things that you know you shouldn't do. If this happens, the first thing you should do is tell an adult you trust.

If that adult doesn't help you, tell another adult. If that adult can't help, ask someone else. It might be hard, but you have to believe that you are worth the effort and that you don't deserve to feel scared at school, in your community, or at home.

In addition to asking an adult for help, try to build some support with your friends. Don't keep what's happening to you a secret. If a kid or a group of kids are bullying you, you can bet they are bullying other kids as well. Maybe you can start an anti-bullying club where you make sure every kid in your class has someone to walk home with, or maybe you can start a "safe" table in the cafeteria that allows anyone who wants to sit there to sit down. Remember, you are not alone. By giving your family and friends a chance to help you, you are allowing them the opportunity to show you how much they love and care for you.

One more topic we have to talk about before we leave the subject of bullies and bullying is how to not be a bully yourself. Most kids who are bullies have been victims of bullies in the past, and taking up the mean-and-tormenting baton is how they try to make themselves feel better. Sometimes girls mistakenly think they're having harmless fun, when the target of their attention isn't having any fun at all.

Anytime you are crossing someone's boundaries (whether that person is a boy or a girl), you are acting like a bully.

For example, just like you have the right to decide who touches your body, everyone else has this same right. You don't have to be hitting or punching someone in order for the touch to be unwanted; kissing, holding someone down, or tickling them when they don't want to be tickled are all examples of this.

You have to be especially careful of this when the amount of power you have is bigger than the amount of power the other person has. For example, it can be harder to say "no" or "stop it" to someone bigger, older, or someone who has more friends standing around.

If other students at school seem to be scared of you, go out of their way to avoid you, or if you have a sense that you get more fear than respect from other kids in your class, it's possible that you've fallen into patterns of acting like a bully. Ask a trusted adult if there is someone you can talk to who can help you with this behavior and can support you having healthy friendships.

Sometimes you can end up behaving like a bully just because you're hanging out with kids that like to torment and tease other kids. Once you watch someone do mean stuff to other students, it starts to become easier to do these same things yourself. Ask a teacher or another adult you trust to help you design an escape plan from the not-so-awesome friend group.

✿ Personal Safety: Maintaining Those Boundaries

It's not fun to listen to grown-ups talk on and on about how dangerous everything is. Let's be real, girls, not everything in the world is dangerous, and certainly not everyone in the world is out to do something bad to kids. However, in order to feel safe and secure, you need to develop certain skills to help you recognize safe and unsafe behavior, and you need to have good boundaries between yourself and the rest of the world.

Another thing that both adults and other kids might do that crosses boundaries is access private information without permission. For example, if your friend picks up your phone and reads your text messages, that is crossing a boundary because they are not respecting your right to privacy. You can tell friends that this behavior is not okay with you and you can also help the people in your life feel safe by not snooping around in their personal emails, texts, or social media messages. If you are worried that there is something that your friend is doing or saying behind your back, finding out about it by reading their private messages won't help the friendship. If you talk with them about your worries, even if what they say hurts your feelings, you'll understand much more clearly and will be able to move forward.

There are things you can do out in the world that will help maintain your boundaries. For example, of course you shouldn't talk with strangers, or get into a car with someone you don't know well, or accept gifts from adults you don't know. You should also make sure not to give any personal information about yourself to people who don't need that information. This includes information you may give out electronically, for example by filling out entry forms for contests or posting personal information online.

If you are home alone after school or while your parents are at work, it's best not to broadcast this fact. Always ask to see the badge or identification card of anyone like a police officer or a gas repair person who comes to the door—you can even check the badge through the peephole, that's what

it is made for! Always check with your parents to see if they are expecting anyone before you open the door. When in doubt, don't open the door; just tell whoever it is to come back again some other time.

✿ Building a Great Reputation and Staying Safe

Whenever you hear a grown-up say, "Mmmm, that person has gotten themselves a reputation," you know they probably don't mean anything good. But just like you can get a reputation with other kids at school, you can also build a good reputation with everyday actions. Even though you can't control what anyone else says about you, you can take steps to build and protect a good reputation.

Why should you care about your reputation? A good reputation is important because it helps people trust you. A girl with a good reputation has an advantage because adults and her friends expect her to be responsible and helpful, instead of expecting her to behave in a negative or a destructive way.

Building a good reputation is all about showing people around you that you have good character. There are lots of things that go into good character, but some of the most important are:

- Being truthful with your friends, family members, and other adults. This is even more important when you have to be honest about doing something that is going to have negative consequences.
- Acting responsibly, especially by doing what you have agreed to do, even when it's hard.
- Having self-control to do boring things when you'd rather do something else will pay off in the long run (like homework).

- Not becoming involved in drama for its own sake. While it's true that what adults call drama girls sometimes think of as "figuring stuff out with your friends," if you want to decrease the drama in your life, the quickest way is to decrease how much you talk about people behind their backs. It can be a hard habit to break at first, but it will make your life much simpler.

❋ Staying Safe in Electronic and Virtual Worlds

The internet can be a pretty amazing place. You can communicate with friends and far-away family members, learn more about your favorite hobbies and interests, play games, learn random trivia tidbits to impress your friends, and watch a lot of videos of cats doing cute things.

The number one thing you need to always remember and never forget is that nothing you post or share in the cyber world (or through any kind of electronic connection) is ever really private.

Before you send that text or photo out there, ask yourself: "Would I be okay with everyone in the whole world knowing what I am saying right now or seeing this picture? Not just the person I am sending this to, but everyone? My family, my teachers, my principal, every single one of my friends, my babysitter when I was four, and even total strangers?"

Even things you post on supposedly anonymous apps or videos that "disappear" after they are watched don't always stay private. Anything can be screenshot or screen-capped, and once it's out there, it's out there forever. You lose control completely; anyone can share it and anyone can pass it around. You've made a digital trail that can continue to follow you long after you've hit send.

The trail doesn't have to be made on purpose to cause you problems; the person you share a photo with can be a best friend who would never ever betray you or share the photo without your permission. But what happens if they lose their phone at school and the photo gets into someone else's hands? Even if it's just a goofy photo of you waking up in the morning with your hair sticking straight up, you might not want everyone in the world to see it.

Also remember: almost everyone you meet online is a stranger. And the trustworthy adults in your life have warned you about talking to strangers, right? If someone you don't  know in real life contacts you online and wants to meet with you, tell a trusted adult. Online, anyone can say they are a kid, or even use someone else's photos to make a fake profile.

If you're playing games online that involve other random players, be especially careful that your screen-name doesn't give away any information, and make sure you know how to report abusive messages or cyberbullying in the game environment.

Also, think carefully before sharing personal information such as locations (for example, "checking in" on different social media sites) or the fact that you're home alone (e.g., "Watching scary movie while fam is out, jumping at every noise LOL") to everyone with a phone or a computer.

It's also important to respect your friends' and family members' boundaries on social media. Talk with your friends about whether it is OK to tag them in photos and check them into locations, and be careful about what you post on their wall or write in response to their posts or shares.

Finally, use hard-to-guess passcodes and change your passcodes frequently. One easy way to make a memorable passcode is use an entire sentence, complete with punctuation, or even switch out some of the letters for numbers. "Il0vemyd0gFid0." is going to be much easier for you to remember (and harder for others to stumble into or figure out) than a string of random numbers or your birthday.

Don't ever use your birthday or your name as your passcode.

❖ Cyberbullying

Cyberbullying is any kind of bullying that takes place using electronic technology like cell phones, tablets, computers, or any other device you can use to get online. Cyberbullying is not that different from everyday, in-person bullying, but at times it can be even more harmful because:

- Cyberbullying can happen anytime, anyplace. You don't have to be anywhere near the person bullying you to feel scared or threatened.
- In the electronic world, things can be spread far and wide in no time at all.
- Cyberbullying can make school bullying worse by continuing it 24 hours a day, 7 days a week.
- People who engage in cyberbullying don't have to see the face of the person they are hurting; this means their bullying behavior can get out of control even faster.

- Online, it's easy to post anonymous information or hide behind a fake profile so bullies don't have to take responsibility for their actions.

So, what can you do about cyberbullying? Like bullying in real life, being the victim of cyberbullies is never your fault. But you can do certain things to protect yourself and the people you care about:

- Say something. If someone is threatening you, spreading rumors about you, sharing your private information, forwarding your messages, or engaging in cyberbullying, immediately screen-cap the bullying content (if possible) and then report them to the application or software for "terms of service" violations. In most apps targeted to kids your age, the report function should be very obvious. If it's possible, block the screen-name and then tell a trusted adult right away. Information and gossip spreads fast on the internet, so acting quickly is important.
- Protect personal information. This means choosing effective passcodes and logging out of your accounts when on a shared computer. It also means not letting yourself be pressured into sharing any photos or information that you don't want to share or that you wouldn't want shared with the whole world!
- Don't participate in cyberbullying yourself in any way, and do your part to protect other kids. This means not pulling out your phone to video kids fighting—find an adult to break it up instead!
- If someone posts something harmful or private about someone, don't "like" it or share it. If you know someone has created a fake profile and is using it to bully, report it or tell an adult you trust.

Being either a victim of a cyberbully or the cyberbully can have really drastic consequences for a girl's future. Some victims of cyberbullying have been forced to change schools or have had to shut down all their social media accounts, and some cyberbullies have been kicked out of school or have even gone to jail. So please keep yourself safe in the cyberworld.

❧ Give Yourself a Break

The beauty of having the world at your fingertips through a smartphone is that you can reach out to anyone you need to, whenever you need to. The drawback is that the world can also reach you!

Especially as you approach your teen years, when you're building your own social groups outside of your family, social contact becomes more of the focus of your daily life, almost like a job. A fun job, but still a job. If you're on your phone 24/7 and available all the time, that's like working around the clock. Even brain surgeons have days off, right?

Here are a few ways you can take charge of your digital life instead of letting it take charge of you:

- Make sure you have real conversations with your friends, not just text conversations. With texts, you have time to think through every interaction, and exactly how it will be understood and what it says about you, but real-time, real-life conversations are more spontaneous and just as fun!

- Set your phone to airplane mode at night, or use the "do not disturb" function. If you're worried about missing an emergency call, you can set the "do not disturb" to allow incoming calls from your favorites or from the same caller within a short time period, like three minutes.

- Have "screen-free" days once in a while. You deserve to have some personal time. You do not have to be instantly available to everyone you know all the time. Maybe being occasionally unavailable will lend you an air of mystery!

- If you feel like you'd like more screen-free time but have trouble removing yourself from your devices, enlist your parents or other trustworthy adults in your fight. Maybe your house can have a "collect and drop" space where you leave your cell phone or tablet before you go to bed or when you're doing your homework. If you have a big paper to work on and you've already done all the online research, ask the adults at home to serve as your site-blocking software and temporarily change the internet password to keep you on task.
- Did you know that social scientists have done research on how social media impacts how we feel every day, and people who spend the most time on social media are actually the most lonely? The researchers developed a theory that being on social media feels like social interaction, but doesn't have all the qualities of hanging out with people in real life. It's like eating cotton candy when you're really hungry instead of sitting down to an actual meal. You can avoid that situation by choosing quality of interaction over quantity of interaction. Instead of belonging to every single social media site, pick one or two that work best for you and limit your "friends" to people you are actually friends with, not people that you have only met once or twice. Use social media to plan for activities in real life, instead of letting it be a substitute for real-life activities.
- Experiment with going to a concert, a movie, or out with friends without taking photos or posting about it on social media. It's a different kind of experience, and you might enjoy it in a different way.

Stressed is Desserts Spelled Backward

Every girl's brain and body are different from every other girl's brain and body, that's a fact. In fact, that's what makes you, well, you! And just like every girl is different, every girl has her very own strengths and weaknesses, or things she does well and things she struggles with. Some of these things you'll notice when doing schoolwork. For example, some girls might be great writers, able to complete 10-page papers with no problem, while others find a two-sentence assignment a huge challenge. You might notice some differences during sports, where there are some girls who are better athletes without even having to try very hard.

❁ All Different Bodies, All Different Brains

Some differences are just part of how a girl's body functions. For example, some girls with ADHD (Attention Deficit Hyperactivity Disorder) might have trouble sitting still and concentrating. In order to function well in school, these girls might need to take prescription medication to focus and finish their work.

If you're one of those girls, it's important to remember there's not something wrong with your brain, your brain just works a little differently.

Sometimes girls have brains that make it hard for them to understand what people mean when they say things, or to understand how friendships and conversations work. Sometimes girls who have brains that work in that specific way are said to have ASD (Autism Spectrum Disorder). They might take medication, they might need to be told things in a certain way, or they might need to be in a classroom that is run in a way that helps their brain work best.

These differences in how different girls' brains and bodies work don't have to be stressful. When the differences do cause stress, it's usually because people in the bigger world haven't spent any time thinking about how they can make sure their part of the world is accessible to people whose brains and bodies might work differently.

For example, a girl might have a body that works a little differently than other kids in her class: instead of walking, she might use a wheelchair to get around. If she lives in a house that is all on one floor with a ramp to the front door, she might not be stressed about using a wheelchair until she shows up for the first day of high school and discovers that there is a huge flight of stairs just to get into the school! Clearly, it's not the wheelchair stressing the girl out; it's the lack of thinking by the people at her school that's causing the stress.

If you've been stressed out by the difference between the way your brain or body works and the way the rest of the world works, remember that everyone has their own challenges. No one's brain or body is perfect, no matter how it might appear to an outsider. Every single person on earth struggles with something, so make sure to take the time to learn about other people and know you're not alone.

What should you do if a girl who has a brain or body that might not work exactly like yours has a class with you or rides the bus with you or is in a community group with you? You might feel a little uncertain about how to treat that kid, but there isn't any one way to talk to her because each girl is an individual and each situation is different. Just think about how you'd want to be treated and follow their lead. If you think the girl might want some help with something, ask if you can help, and make sure you listen closely to her answer—don't assume what anyone can or can't do!

You probably know this already, but ignoring or teasing kids who are different than you won't make you (or them) feel good. Every person has feelings, and every girl wants to have friends and be liked. You might find that if you go a little bit out of your way to befriend a kid whose brain or body works differently, that you might be the one who gains the most from the friendship.

❁ Moving

Moving can be a very stressful time in a girl's life. When your parents first tell you that you are going to move, you might be mad. The idea might take some getting used to. After a while, you might want to take some steps that will help you think about how the move might be good for you and for your family. Here are a few first steps:

- Look up your new town online. What is near your house? Is there anything fun there that you couldn't do in your current neighborhood? Google Maps may let you get a 360° view of your new street, neighborhood, and town.
- Look up your new school online and see if you can memorize the names of the teachers and their pictures. That way you can be the new kid who knows all the teachers' names the first time you see them!
- Plan how you want to decorate your new room, and maybe even use some of the more grown-up styles you've been thinking about.
- If you're going to move in the summer, ask if you can join a community sports league, go to activities at the local community center, or visit the local library to meet some kids. That way you don't have to wait until school starts to make friends.

As with most things in life, you'll likely discover that there are both good and bad things about moving. The bad things you've probably already thought about yourself, so here are some good things to keep in mind on this new adventure:

- This is an opportunity to reinvent yourself. No one at your new school knows anything about you. No one knows that you blew the big game, tripped in the hallway, or forgot all your lines in the school play in first grade. You can build yourself a brand-new reputation as the person you want to be.
- You get to make new friends. Choose carefully and you'll probably find friends who will help you navigate all the hard parts of growing up.
- Here's a chance to get closer to your parents and siblings.

Since they will be the only ones you know at first, use the time to hang out with them. Play games, explore your neighborhood, and build up your connections to the people who love you most.

❧ Divorce

Although it isn't always as dramatic as it seems on TV, divorce can also be very hard on kids. The most important thing to remember if your parents are getting divorced: it is never, ever, ever (are you listening?) the kids' fault. Divorce is a choice adults make for adult reasons. Even if you were super extra good and never teased your little sister again, or if you were super extra bad and made her life completely miserable, you couldn't cause (or prevent) your parents' divorce.

When parents break up, there is often a lot of shuffling around of kids, and you may have to adjust to having two homes instead of one, or even (later) having a new stepparent or stepsiblings. This can be really difficult, especially at first. If you are having trouble with this, it's important to talk with your parents directly, rather than acting out your feelings with bad behavior. With bad behavior you might get the attention you want, but it will be negative—not positive—attention.

Divorce is one of the most stressful things a kid can deal with, but there are ways to make the situation as easy as it can be. Here are a few tips:

- Divorce is more difficult for a family if the parents can't get along at all. Remind your parents that they can have their disagreements when you are not around.
- Accept that some changes will happen. You may have to change schools or even move. You'll get used to your life sooner if you try to look at the positive aspects of it.

- Some families have money problems as parents try to adjust to having two homes and two lives instead of one. You may have to change your spending habits and your expectations of gifts at special occasions.
- Talk to someone. Don't keep your feelings inside—there are people out there who care about you and want to help.

❊ Drugs, Alcohol and Other Unhealthy Stuff

Hopefully, you are looking at this and thinking, "Why are they talking about this? I am way too young to even think about stuff like that." Unfortunately that's not true for all girls. In fact, 6 percent of all kids your age say they drink alcohol on a regular basis.

Even if you don't see many people in your life smoking, drinking alcohol, or using illegal drugs, you are still exposed to advertising for alcohol and tobacco products. You have probably seen movies and TV shows that show people using illegal drugs, so you probably know some things about alcohol and drugs, even if they haven't touched your life directly.

The best place to get information about smoking, drugs, and alcohol is from an adult you trust. They especially need to know if someone asks you to try these things. It's important—but not always easy—to say "no" to drugs.

It's especially hard if there are lots of drugs around you. If this is true for you, talk with the adults that are responsible for taking care of you about changing things in your environment (like where you live, where you go to school and what adults you are around) to help you stay drug-free. Even if you can't move or change schools, they can help you think up ways to make your environment safer—by changing how you walk to school or finding different activities to be involved in after school, for example.

One of the ways girls are pressured to use drugs is by someone presenting drinking, smoking, or getting high as an adult thing to do. But facing your problems head on, and being "in the moment" (instead of being tuned out by illegal substances) is the best way to show how grown-up you are.

❁ Super Stressed Families

Every family has stress, but some families have much more stress to deal with than others. For example, some families have to cope with having very little money, someone in the family drinking too much or using drugs, homelessness, or living in a neighborhood with a lot of crime.

Sometimes (but not always) situations like this make it hard for the adults in the family to be consistent with discipline and providing for kids' needs, even if they are trying very hard. Sometimes these adults need help so that they can be the kind of parents they want to be.

If you are afraid of someone in your family, aren't getting your basic needs (clothing, food, going to the doctor) met, or your family is super stressed in some way, it's very important that you talk to someone. Your school guidance counselor or school nurse can be good people to start with. It might be really hard to ask for help, but it is very brave. Often super stressed families have many strengths; they just need help getting back on track.

To Your Future and Beyond!

You've grown a lot already—probably even since you started reading this book—but you still have even more growing to do. While growing up may be difficult at times, keep in mind that you only have to go through the process of puberty once in your lifetime. Remember that all the experiences of growing up—the good, the bad, the happy, the sad—are what will make you into the person you are meant to be.

Finally, know this: there is no one perfect way to be a girl! Some girls like roses and pink princess T-shirts, and some girls think pink princess T-shirts are the worst. Some girls like to play the drums on a drill team, and some girls like to play the flute. Some girls never want to get dirty, while some girls think getting dirty is the best. None of these ways to be a girl is wrong!

Respect the girl you are inside and say good things to yourself. You're on your way to being a strong, amazing woman, so don't forget to celebrate yourself today and every day!

Index

Index

Index

About Applesauce Press

Good ideas ripen with time. From seed to harvest, Applesauce Press creates books with beautiful designs, creative formats, and kid-friendly information. Like our parent company, Cider Mill Press Book Publishers, our press bears fruit twice a year, publishing a new crop of titles each spring and fall.

"Where Good Books Are Ready for Press"

Visit us on the web at
cidermillpress.com
or write to us at
12 Spring Street, PO Box 454
Kennebunkport, Maine 04046